Th Locomotive Giggleswick

LMS Patriot Class No. 5538

Nigel Mussett

Kirkdale Publications
2003

Published by Kirkdale Publications 2003
Kirkdale, Station Road, Giggleswick,
Settle, North Yorkshire. BD24 0AB

ISBN 0 907089 04 6

Printed by Lamberts Print and Design
Station Road, Settle, North Yorkshire. BD24 9AA

*Dedicated to the memory of
my friend and colleague O. S. Nock ('Ossie'),
railway signal engineer and doyen of railway authors,
English gentleman and
one of Giggleswick's most famous sons,
and of his wife Olivia,
a most gracious lady, a kindly and generous hostess.*

The left nameplate prior to the official naming ceremony 1938. *National Railway Museum*

The right nameplate, having been unveiled, awaits the formal naming with champagne at Settle Station, 4 November 1938. *Richard Holt Collection*

Contents

Official photograph of LMS No. 5538 *Giggleswick* proudly displaying its new name outside the paint shops on 27 October 1938 prior to its journey to Settle for the formal naming ceremony eight days later. *National Railway Museum*

Acknowledgements

I wish to acknowledge the help of many people over several years in compiling material relating to the locomotive *Giggleswick*. Soon after I first encountered the nameplate at Giggleswick School in 1973 it was not long before I met one of the school's most famous Old Boys, Ossie Nock. As our friendship developed, he took great delight in demonstrating the running of his scale model of the locomotive in his renowned railway house at Batheaston. At about the same time Philip Leadbeater of Settle showed me some long-forgotten photographs of the naming ceremony taken by his brother and copies were soon obtained by courtesy of *The Yorkshire Post*.

Throughout my researches this year I have been able to trace many more photographs and I am grateful for the readiness and frequent generosity with which copyright holders have made available images in their possession and for their permission to include these in this collection. For convenience, credits are acknowledged individually with each caption. Staff at the National Railway Museum, and in particular Lynne Thurston, Edward Bartholomew, Phil Atkins and Martin Bashforth, have provided practical help in my researches and been patient with my numerous requests. Nelson Twells of the LMS Society has given generously of his time providing information and reviewing the final proof. Gordon Coltas, Mark Hoofe, Barry Hoper and Brian Stephenson have contributed much during the course of our conversations as well as enabling me to draw upon the wealth of photographs in their possession; nothing has been too much trouble for these dedicated enthusiasts and I thank them for their interest and for sharing their knowledge.

My colleagues at Giggleswick School have also taken a keen interest in the project: John Mounsey, Deputy Bursar and fellow railway enthusiast, has shared details of contacts made through the school and Adele Foster allowed me to photograph her Hornby model in black livery. To Mike Howarth we are indebted for drawing the school's attention to the existence of the British Pathe newsreel footage of the naming ceremony in 1938.

I should also like to acknowledge the assistance and ready co-operation given by Ian Wright of Sheffield Railwayana Auctions. To Mrs Pamela Barton I owe a debt of gratitude for putting me in contact with Edward Hickling whose contribution to the *Giggleswick* story has been particularly significant.

Dr David Hucknall, another long-standing friend and associate, gave me instant answers to some simple questions which for some reason were not evident elsewhere. It has been a pleasure working on the commemorative display board with Glynn Hague of the Friends of the Settle-Carlisle Line and Tim Parker, Arriva Retail Supervisor at Settle Station. The contributions made by four individuals who were present at the naming ceremony, namely Edward Hickling, Richard Holt, Gregory McIntosh and Joan Roberts (née Bilsborough), are particularly noteworthy and have provided us with an unrivalled link with the past.

I wish also to thank Ken Hill, our professional photographer in Settle, for the care and efficiency with which he has printed many of the illustrations for me and also Chris Burgon and his team at Lamberts Print and Design for the patience and expert guidance which they have all given in seeing the book into print.

Finally, in acknowledging assistance from all of these quarters I must, however, claim full responsibility for any remaining errors or omissions. If, by some oversight, there are any then I apologise and crave the reader's forbearance.

Introduction

The London, Midland and Scottish Railway locomotive No. 5538 *Giggleswick* was built in 1933 and subsequently named after the Yorkshire public school at which I was privileged to teach for twenty nine years. The decision by the Governors of Giggleswick School to sell one of the locomotive's nameplates in 2003 by public auction sparked a renewed interest in the engine amongst members of the school and railway enthusiasts alike. Prior to the auction several full-size brass replica nameplates were made and a series of Gauge 00 models, using the current Hornby design, had been commissioned by the school. This now seems an appropriate occasion on which to bring together as much material about the locomotive as I possess in the form of this modest publication.

As a result of announcements concerning the auctioning of the nameplate, several kind people who in one way or another had been associated with the locomotive have come forward with further photographs and their own particular memories of the famous engine. No doubt there are still many others who could add further details to the story and inevitably there will be other photographs of *Giggleswick* which have escaped my notice. The locations of the left nameplate, the smokebox numberplates and work's plate are not known. Some or all of these are possibly in private collections. Several tantalising questions remain to be answered, particularly with regard to changes in livery, despite extensive research.

Nevertheless, it is time to go to print and I hope that this little volume will be of interest to the wide fraternity of those who hold fond memories of the locomotive, the railway and the school which it represented for nearly thirty years.

N. J. Mussett
Giggleswick
November 2003

LNWR 'Claughton' Class No. 1191 *Sir Frank Ree* **at Camden sheds, north London. Originally built in May 1913, this locomotive and the name it carried played a pivotal role in the history of the LMS 'Patriot' Class.** *National Railway Museum*

GWR No. 5000 *Launceston Castle* **at Tyseley motive power depot, Birmingham, in 1930. The experimental use of this engine by the LMS in 1926 led directly to the development of the 'Royal Scot' Class, on which the design of the 'Patriots' was subsequently based.** *Locofotos*

1. Development of the 'Patriots'

The 'Patriot' Class of locomotives evolved by a complicated process of hybridisation, almost unlike any other in the history of British locomotive design. Details of the technical and 'political' aspects of the developments which led to the appearance of the 'Patriots' are widely discussed in the literature but a brief outline of the main events involved will help place this popular class of locomotives in its historical context. The limited selection of photographs which accompanies this chapter will, I hope, help to illustrate visually the progression of locomotive design and some of the individual engines involved in the complex history of the 'Patriots'.

Our story commences in the mid-1920s when Sir Henry Fowler was appointed Chief Mechanical Engineer of the London, Midland and Scottish Railway. Fowler had begun working on a grand project to build a four-cylinder compound Pacific 4-6-2 locomotive much along the lines of a successful French design of the time. His plan proved unpopular and he was instructed to stop work on the project which was already under way in 1926.

When the amalgamation or grouping of the various private railway companies took place in 1923 to form what were known as 'The Big Four' (LMS, LNER, GWR and SR)[1], the LMS had inherited a large class of 130 powerful (for the time) but far from ideal main line four-cylindered 4-6-0 locomotives from the former London and North Western Railway (LNWR) known as the 'Claughtons'. This design of engine had taken its name from the first one of the class to be built, No. 2222, and bearing the name *Sir Gilbert Claughton*, one-time Chairman of the LNWR. The 'Claughtons' were built between 1913 and 1921 and had been allocated numbers as they were built wherever there was a gap in the company's list. Under the LMS in 1923 they were renumbered sequentially from 5900 to 6029 inclusive according to their date of construction. It was, however, not long before the LMS began searching for ideas for possible successors to the 'Claughtons'. Designs from rival railway companies were considered and late in 1926 the GWR 4-6-0 No. 5000 *Launceston Castle* went on loan for some experimental running with the LMS. So impressive was the performance of

---

1. London, Midland and Scottish Railway; London and North Eastern Railway; Great Western Railway and Southern Railway.

No. 5000 in these trials that Sir Henry Fowler was instructed to get fifty comparable locomotives built to a new design, but with only three cylinders, in time for the summer working of 1927. Strange to say, earlier exchanges of engines between railway companies in 1909-1910 had resulted in the LNWR being influenced to some extent by the fine performance of an earlier GWR design in the development of its own 'Claughton' Class.

Fowler's new three-cylinder locomotives were built by the North British Locomotive Company in Glasgow and were destined to haul the heavy Anglo-Scottish express services, including the prestigious 'Royal Scot' service, on the west coast main line as serious rivals to the 'Flying Scotsman' east coast services operated by the LNER. The leading locomotive of the new class was given the number 6100 and later appropriately named *Royal Scot*, thereby giving its name to the class as a whole. Others followed throughout the rest of the year and their performance was impressive from the outset, although constant improvements were made in the years ahead. In all, seventy 'Royal Scots' were built at this time. According to O.S. Nock (1978), they initially had a tractive effort of 33,150lb but Derek Cross (1982) claims that this was

LMS 'Royal Scot' Class No. 6163 *Civil Service Rifleman* in its original form. This locomotive was rebuilt in 1953 with a 2A tapered boiler and was finally withdrawn in 1964. *Gordon Tidey/National Railway Museum*

achieved in their later rebuilt form with the Stanier Type 2A boiler; their working boiler pressure was 250lb/sq. in., giving them a power rating of Class 6.

Meanwhile, however, it was decided that the LMS also required a batch of second-line 3-cylinder 4-6-0 express passenger locomotives. Eyes were cast back to the 'Claughtons'. As some of these ageing and not wholly successful engines were approaching the end of their lives, it was deemed possible, probably for accounting reasons, to rebuild them as slightly smaller versions of the 'Royal Scots', again, with only three cylinders.

Opportunity was therefore taken of using two damaged 'Claughtons', LMS No. 5971 Croxteth and LMS No. 5902 Sir Frank Ree, for the first of the new hybrid prototypes reconstructed at the former Midland Railway's Derby works in November 1930. O.S. Nock (1978) states that the original driving wheels of these two locomotives, with their large central bosses, were incorporated into the old frames but the wheel spacing was altered. The front bogie, the reversing gear and the whistle were also reused whilst the cylinders, valves and valve gear were identical to those used on the new 'Royal Scots'. The enlarged Belpaire G9.5S parallel boiler, fitted to twenty of the 'Claughtons' from 1928, had proved successful and it operated at a pressure of 200lb/sq. in., giving the engines a tractive effort of over 27,000lb and a power rating in Class 5X as opposed to the Class 5 of the unmodified 'Claughtons' and Class 6 of the 'Royal Scots' at that time. In the two reconstructed 'Claughtons', Nos 5971 and 5902, the G9.5S boiler and associated mechanical gear gave the locomotives a now slightly reduced tractive effort of 26,520lb, but still within a Class 5X rating. For this reason the new class was officially termed 'Class 5X Three-cylinder (converted) Claughton'. Not without good reason, however, was this new hybrid locomotive more conveniently and affectionately dubbed by railwaymen as a 'Baby Scot' or, by those north of the Border, a 'Wee Scot'. The tender attached to these locomotives, as to the 'Royal Scots', was the standard 3,500-gallon type in use at the time which also carried 5.5 tons of coal.

The rebuilt No. 5971 was sent to Leeds Holbeck shed and proved its worth over the Settle-Carlisle line in the early 1930s where, incidentally, it had been badly damaged in the collision which fatefully made it readily available for conversion. No. 5902 worked out of Crewe and proved itself over Shap. It was apparent that the 'Baby Scot' design offered an immediate solution to the problem of providing further passenger Class 5X locomotives

Former LNWR 'Claughton' No. 2511, built in June 1920 and shown here in 1923 after being renumbered 5971 and named *Croxteth* under the LMS. This was the first passenger locomotive to be repainted in LMS crimson livery following the regrouping earlier that year. Note the small lettering as first used by the LMS. *National Railway Museum*

LMS No. 5902 *Sir Frank Ree* at Nottingham Midland station on 11 August 1932 after its conversion in 1930 from LNWR 'Claughton' No. 1191 into a 'Baby Scot'. The similarity between this locomotive and the slightly larger 'Royal Scots' is apparent. *T.G. Hepburn/Rail Archive Stephenson*

until more powerful engines were developed under the new LMS Chief Mechanical Engineer William Stanier, appointed in 1932. To this end a further forty 'Claughton' Class locomotives were ordered to be converted into 'Baby Scots'. These engines utilised only a minimum of old parts but on a new 'Royal Scot' type of chassis. The first fifteen of them to appear were built at the former LNWR works at Crewe in 1932, as were a further fifteen (of which No. 6000 – later No. 5538 *Giggleswick* – was one) in 1933. The remaining ten engines were built at Derby, also in 1933, and still using some parts from the old 'Claughtons'. A final ten were built entirely new at Crewe in 1934, bringing the total in the 'Baby Scot' Class to fifty two. Scrapping of the unconverted 'Claughtons' began in 1932 and continued until 1949, the last one being BR No. 46004, formerly No. 42 under the LNWR and renumbered 6004 under the LMS.

In 1934 the LMS took the opportunity of introducing a logical

LMS No. 5971 poses on the turntable at Nottingham Midland carriage sidings. As the former LNWR 'Claughton' Class No. 2511 *Croxteth*, it was renumbered by the LMS at the time of the grouping in 1923 and was one of the two prototypes selected for conversion into 'Baby Scots' in November 1930. The large central wheel bosses of the original engine are evident in this photograph but its nameplates were not added until 1933 (note the exposed backplate above the front wheel splasher). Then it was renumbered LMS No. 5500 in 1934 as leader of the new 'Baby Scot' Class.
T.G. Hepburn/Rail Archive Stephenson

renumbering scheme to all of its locomotives. Unconverted 'Claughtons' kept their 1923 LMS numbers but members of the 'Baby Scot' Class were renumbered sequentially from 5500 to 5551 inclusive. No. 6000 became No. 5538 on 3 August 1934. Before we trace the story of our dedicated locomotive No. 5538 we must first recall how the term 'Patriot' came to be given to the class as a whole.

One of the 'Claughtons', built in 1920, had been given the number 1914 and named *Patriot* in honour of the railwaymen of the London and North Western Railway who had died in World War 1. It carried an impressive set of large nameplates to this effect until it was scrapped in July 1934, having been renumbered 5964 by the LMS at the time of the grouping in 1923. Meanwhile, the first 'Claughton' to be rebuilt in 1930 and converted to a 'Baby Scot', No. 5971 *Croxteth*, did not have its name transferred until 1933. This engine then became No. 5500 in the new LMS numbering scheme of 1934 and, by virtue of being numerically first in the list, became

'Claughton' Class No. 1914 *Patriot* in plain black livery at Crewe, 22 May 1920. This was the LNWR war memorial engine and it carried huge nameplates bearing the additional inscription: "In memory of the fallen L & NWR employees 1914-1919". It entered service in May 1920, was renumbered No. 5964 by the LMS in 1923 and finally withdrawn in July 1934. *National Railway Museum*

leader of the new 'Baby Scot' or '5500' Class. It did, however, continue to carry the name *Croxteth* until February 1937 when it was decided to rename it *Patriot*, taking over the name from the now withdrawn 'Claughton' LMS No. 5964. Thus the commemorative name, if not the number, of the former LNWR war memorial engine was ultimately perpetuated by the first of the 'Baby Scots' and, in consequence, by the class as a whole. As BR No. 45500, *Patriot* was withdrawn and broken up in March 1961.

In April 1937, No. 5971's companion, former LNWR 'Claughton' No. 5902 *Sir Frank Ree*, now 'Patriot' Class No. 5501, was appropriately renamed *St Dunstan's* in honour of the home founded in 1915 for servicemen who had lost their sight in the First World War. The name *Sir Frank Ree* was then transferred to 'Patriot' No. 5530 which was destined to be the last member of the class to be withdrawn from service in December 1965.

LMS 'Baby Scot' No. 5500, formerly *Croxteth*, renamed *Patriot* on 25 February 1937, taking over the name from the former 'Claughton' No. 1914 (later, LMS No. 5964) which had been scrapped in July 1934. It had been renumbered No. 5500 in 1934 and so became the leader of the 'Baby Scot' Class. Once acquiring its new name, 'Patriot' became the official name of the '5500' or 'Baby Scot' Class as a whole, of which No. 5538 *Giggleswick* was a member. *National Railway Museum*

LMS No. 5530 *Sir Frank Ree*, having taken over this name from LMS No. 5501 when that engine was renamed *St Dunstan's* in April 1937. Like *Giggleswick*, No. 5530 had been a 1933 rebuild of a former 'Claughton' (being originally LNWR No. 205, built June 1921). It became LMS No. 6022 on the grouping in 1923 and carried this number in its rebuilt form until being renumbered LMS No. 5530 in the 1934 scheme. It was then destined to be one of the 18 'Patriots' to be rebuilt as shown here with a Stanier Type 2A type tapered boiler and given an enlarged tender. Curved smoke deflectors were added later. *National Railway Museum*

BR No. 45530 *Sir Frank Ree*, photographed under the wires at Crewe in its final rebuilt form with the tapered 2A boiler and curved smoke deflectors. Rebuilt in October 1946, it was the last member of the 'Patriot' Class to be withdrawn in December 1965. *Locofotos*

2. Years with the LMS: 1933-1947

The rebuild of LMS No. 6000 from the former LNWR 'Claughton' No. 15 at Crewe works was completed on 21 July 1933. Only the original reversing screw, whistle and possibly the bogie wheels were incorporated into what was otherwise a new engine. The locomotive was finished in LMS crimson livery, elegantly lined in black and yellow. The number was shown on the cab whilst the tender, No. 4510, bore the company's initials 'LMS'. At this stage, of course, the engine was unnamed. The cost of reconstruction is given on the Engine History Card as £5223.12.6d and the tender as £832. The locomotive was at first allocated to the Midland Division of the LMS on 30 October and hauled passenger trains both north (over the Settle-Carlisle line) and south from Leeds Holbeck motive power depot. It will be recalled that the locomotive was renumbered 5538 on 3 August 1934 under the new LMS scheme. On 16 February 1935 it was re-allocated to Longsight depot (shed code 9A), near Manchester, in the Western Division but by 25 July of the following year it was back in Leeds where it remained throughout World War 2.

Various light repairs were carried out in the pre-war period, including some obviously minor ones relating to damage sustained in a collision. A replacement boiler was fitted in 1935 and at some stage side draught windows were fitted onto the outside of the cab of this and other 'Baby Scots'. It is not apparent what the heavy repairs were in 1935 but they must have been substantial, costing £1077, nearly one fifth of the cost of the rebuild two years earlier and which kept the engine out of service for nearly six weeks. Six more replacement boilers, most of them taken and overhauled from other members of the class, were fitted between 1936 and 1947 whilst it was stabled at Leeds Holbeck (shed code 20A, later 55A).

The Engine History Cards give details of further repairs and mileages covered and lend themselves for detailed analysis by those interested in such matters. To those unfamiliar with steam motive power, it may come as a surprise to observe how many days each year a typical locomotive may be out of service for routine maintenance as well as for repairs. *Giggleswick* covered a total of 857,524 miles during her LMS days since she entered service in July 1933 until the end of 1947; this represents an average of 57,168 miles per year, running for an average of 76.4% of the days of the year.

LMS locomotive No. 6000 nearing the completion of its rebuild from the former 'Claughton' in the erecting shop at Crewe works, July 1933. *Colling Turner/Photomatic – Rail Archive Stephenson*

'Baby Scot' LMS No. 5538 (the future *Giggleswick* and as yet unnamed) at Carlisle Upperby, July 1936, three years after entering new service as a rebuild of the former unnamed LNWR 'Claughton' Class No. 15 locomotive originating from January 1921. Under the LMS, the locomotive had been renumbered No. 6000 in 1923 and was one of the thirty to be converted into a 'Baby Scot'. She became No. 5538 in the new 1934 LMS scheme. *GSL/David Parry Collection*

LMS No. 5538 seen at Derby works where it went for some repairs on 29 May 1937. *J.A. Whaley/Transport Treasury*

LMS 'Baby Scot' Class No. 5538 hauling an express near Sandbach. The engine still bears no nameplates and so the photograph pre-dates late October 1938. *Locofotos*

LMS No. 5538 *Giggleswick* **heading an express at Townthorns, near Rugby, c. 1947.** *Locofotos*

Ian Sixsmith (2003) gives a comprehensive analysis of the 'Patriots' and full biographical details of all fifty two members of the class, accompanied by a superb collection of photographs. As a guide to the type of repairs recorded on the Engine History Cards from which much of his data has been compiled, he gives the following explanations of some of the abbreviations used:

EO	*Engine Order (some jobs seemingly ordered "out of the normal run of things")*
HG	*Heavy General*
HO	*Heavy Overhaul*
HS	*Heavy Service (= HI Heavy Intermediate under BR)*
LC	*Light Casual*
LO	*Light Overhaul*
LS	*Light Service (= LI Light Intermediate under BR)*
NC	*Non-classified*
Rect	*Rectification (involving a short check following a major repair: "tightening up bits that had come loose and loosening bits that were too tight")*

It is at this point in the story that we must focus on how LMS No. 5538 came to acquire the name *Giggleswick*. By coincidence, the Vice-President of the LMS, Brigadier-General Sir Harold Hartley, FRS, was Chief Guest at Giggleswick School's annual Speech Day on 2 July 1938. After presenting the prizes, Sir Harold concluded by saying that the LMS was extremely proud of its engines and that they were named after queens, princesses and famous regiments. In the 'Patriot' or 'Baby Scot' Class there remained a gap to be filled; he thought that it could be arranged to give one of the Leeds-based 'Patriots' the name *Giggleswick*. The offer was readily taken up and in proposing a vote of thanks to Sir Harold, Mr Geoffrey Dawson, at that time one of the school governors and editor of *The Times*, declared that he felt sure that the offer of naming an engine after the school would be accepted. It would help to put Giggleswick on the map – certainly the railway map – to an extent not known since the total eclipse of the sun in 1927 when the village was at the centre of totality and the Astronomer Royal had come to set up his instruments in the field next to the school chapel. 'We shall be extremely grateful for our engine,' added Mr Dawson.

The Southern Railway had introduced a 'Schools' Class of 4-4-0 locomotives in 1930, all named after famous public schools. In 1938 the LMS had not named any of its locomotives after a school (although there is no obvious reason why it should have done so) and so after some hints in the Vice-President's ear on Speech Day, plans were made for the omission to be rectified. The locomotive chosen to bear the name *Giggleswick* was No. 5538. After a repaint and the fixing of the nameplates, with the brass letters of the name contrasting well against the background which was in the LMS's favoured finish of black, the locomotive was lined up outside the paint shop for its official photographs on 27 October 1938. According to O.S. Nock (1974), these photographs were the ones which were usually produced by the railway publicity department when an illustration representative of the 'Patriot' Class was asked for.

The formal naming ceremony at Settle Station took place on Friday 4 November 1938. The LMS went to great lengths to provide a memorable spectacle; the station buildings were decked with bunting and a temporary platform for the railway and school dignitaries was erected on the right side of the locomotive. Film crews and other photographers were out in force. Coverage was given in the local, county and national press. British Pathe News captured the occasion on film, much to the delight of the pupils who, it is said, were as much interested in being filmed as observing the events unfolding before them. Boys and staff walked the mile over from Giggleswick School and were privileged to have a close-up view of the proceedings; members of the public and the local girls' grammar school were kept behind a cordon. The young Edward Hickling, whose father was Foreman at Settle Gas Works, witnessed the occasion amongst the crowd. It was a day he was never to forget and little did he realise that, even after joining the LMS shortly afterwards, he would one day drive the gleaming locomotive now standing before him, or live to share his experiences with the author sixty five years later.

On the platform were Mr H.A. Hicks, District Passenger Manager of the LMS, who presided over the occasion in the absence of Sir Harold Hartley; Mr J.A. Slingsby, Chairman of the Governors; the Headmaster, Mr Edward H. Partridge; and the two youngest boys in the school, eight-year-olds Michael Foster and Gregory McIntosh. In his short speech, Mr Partridge expressed his delight in having an engine named after the school – 'so handsome, powerful and swift an ambassador,' he added. 'I name this locomotive *Giggleswick*. I wish it good luck and may it always be on time!' A bottle of champagne was broken over the right nameplate after the red curtain had been drawn back by

The public naming ceremony at Settle Station, Friday 4 November 1938. The Headmaster of Giggleswick School, Mr Edward H. Partridge, ready to release the bottle of champagne and officially name the LMS locomotive No. 5538 *Giggleswick*. The curtains had just been pulled back by the youngest boys in the school, eight-year-olds Michael Foster (obscured from view) and Gregory McIntosh, seen standing on the right by the nameplate. The Chairman of the Governors, Mr J.A. Slingsby, is seated on the far left of the picture. *Yorkshire Post*

The scene at Settle Station after the naming ceremony. Boys from Giggleswick School were permitted to inspect the locomotive at close quarters by filing through the cab on specially built platforms and steps. *Yorkshire Post*

A general view of the naming ceremony from the embankment opposite Settle Station on the afternoon of Friday 4 November 1938. *Yorkshire Post*

Boys from Giggleswick School line up to view their newly-named locomotive. The LMS had gone to great lengths to decorate the station forecourt; members of the public were able to view events from the rear. Press and newsreel photographers were out in force. *Richard Holt Collection*

Foster and McIntosh. Once the formalities were over, members of the school were invited to inspect the cab and other parts of the locomotive at close quarters. Another platform and pair of steps had been built on the left side of the cab so that boys could file through from one side to the other. Meanwhile, the locomotive gently hissed and steamed, in the charge of Driver W.R. Thompson and Fireman C.E. Short, who apparently had recently driven the Royal Train for King George VI.

During the Second World War the pristine passenger liveries gradually became less obvious as layer upon layer of soot and grime obscured the pre-war colours and, to many, this may have given the impression of a war-time black livery. The war effort swallowed up huge amounts of money and the prime objective of the railway companies was to channel funds into essential maintenance in order to keep the trains running. Repairing locomotives was an obvious and essential requirement and many engines were returned to traffic without having been given a full repaint. More often than not, a touch-up in plain unlined black was given to protect the metal, with pre-war style insignia, letters and numerals from pre-war stocks of transfers being used or the old transfer outlines themselves being painted over in unshaded yellow. Cab windows were blacked out. The result was that war-time locomotives generally looked very drab.

Unfortunately, paint shop records do not seem to have survived and no photographs have been found showing *Giggleswick* during her war-time service. Careful examination of photographs taken in the immediate post-war period, however, certainly suggests that the locomotive had at some stage been painted unlined black during the war and given the simplified LMS numbers on its cab. Whether *Giggleswick* had her nameplates finished in red during the war as was prescribed is not known. In 1946, however, a new post-war LMS livery was adopted in which express passenger locomotives were painted a smart black gloss with maroon and straw-coloured lining and bordered lettering in the Gill *sans serif* style. The cab side numbers were also bordered in the same style with the nameplate being finished in maroon. *Giggleswick* apparently acquired her post-war LMS passenger livery in 1947, but this was to change again after nationalisation.

LMS No. 5538 *Giggleswick* at Kentish Town motive power depot, London. The locomotive is painted in the 1946 post-war LMS livery which it acquired c. 1947. *Locofotos*

LMS No. 5538 *Giggleswick* at Corkerhill depot, Glasgow, in her post-war, prenationalisation 1946 LMS livery. At this time, *Giggleswick* was still allocated to Leeds Holbeck; the shed code 20A is visible on the smokebox door beneath the numberplate. *Locofotos*

Top edge labels (column headers): PASS, GOODS, SHUNTING, TENDER, SUPERHEATER, NON SUPER, N MOTOR, ELECTRIC, 4-2-2, 0-4-0, 0-4-2, 2-4-0, 0-4-4, 2-4-2, 4-4-0, 4-4-2, 4-4-4, 0-6-0, 0-6-2, 4-6-0, 2-6-0, 2-6-2, 2-6-4, 4-6-2, 4-6-4, 0-8-0, 0-8-2, 0-8-4, 2-8-0, 0-10-0

LMS ENGINE HISTORY CARD

RE-NUMBERED **5538**

(CME)

DIVISION **MIDLAND** ~~WESTERN~~ ~~MIDLAND~~ (16-2-35) (1-8-36)   NUMBER ~~6000~~

PASSENGER TENDER ~~————~~ SUPERHEATER   CLASS (MP) **5X**   NAME OR No OF TYPE **3 CYLINDER CLAUGHTON**

WHEEL TYPE **4-6-0**   WHEEL BASE (E & T) **52' 3½"**

EMPTY WEIGHT **75 7** (T C)   WORKING WEIGHT **80 15** (T C)   DIA OF DRIVING WHEELS **6' 9"**

CYLINDERS No. **3**   DIA **18"**   STROKE **26"**   OVERALL LENGTH OVER BUFFERS (E & T) **62' 8¾"**

CLASS OF BOILER **BELPAIRE**   TUBES No **129 & 24** STEEL   BOILER PRESSURE **200** LBS

FIREBOX GRATE AREA **30·3 sq. ft.**   TRACTIVE POWER AT 85% **26520 lbs**

BRAKES   Vacuum (Pump Ejector) / Steam   VALVES **PISTON**   MOTION (TYPE) **WALSCHAERT**   CARRIAGE WARMING WITH

BUILT BY **CREWE**   DATE BUILT **21st JULY 1933.**

ENGINE (incldg Pistons £2 & Sup. £260)

COST £ **5,225 12 4** CHARGED TO &c.

COST OF "IMPROVEMENT" £1 6 10 CHARGED TO

DATE "IMPROVED"   TOTAL COST OF "IMPROVED" ENGINE £

REPLACED BY No.

DATE REPLACED & TRANSFERRED TO DUPLICATE STOCK

AMOUNT TRANSFERRED £ _____ FROM _____ A/c TO _____ A/c

DATE TAKEN OUT OF TRAFFIC _____ DATE BROKEN UP _____ SCRAP VALUE _____

CREDITED TO _____ A/c   MILEAGE UP TO DEC. 31st. 1926 _____

BOILER CHANGES **264,823 ✓**

DATE	PARTICULARS OF BOILERS FITTED					PARTICULARS OF BOILERS TAKEN OUT					COST OF REPRS
	VALUE B / F	FROM	DATE NEW	MILEAGE	Belpaire or Round Top	Belpaire or Round Top	HOW DISPOSED OF	RECOVERED VALUE B / F	MILEAGE	
23·4·35	326 344	6.017	Apl. 1929 1935 NEW	230,915	B(W234)	B(W23a)	5509 Stock	231 73	140,015	86
20·4·36	178 341	5975	Mar. 1936 NEW	208,014	B(W23A)	B(W23A)		92 179		87

*N.W.O. 2506 Light Shield Sliding Firedoor   Balr. Rev. Total ... £1 6 10
× NWO. 3681. Side Draught Windows on Outside of Cab.

DISTINCTIVE TENDER No.

NUMBER	DATE FITTED
LMS 4510	21-7-33

RENEWAL PROVISION

YEAR	COST PER TON	ENGINE INCLUDING BOILER			BOILER			ENGINE EXCLDG.	LIFE		ANNUAL PROVISION	
		GROSS COST	NETT RES DL VALUE	NETT COST	GROSS COST	NETT RES DL VALUE	NETT COST	NETT R.PLACEMENT COST	ENGINE EXCLDG BOILER (YRS)	BOILER (YRS)	ENGINE	BOILER
1933	65·54	4941	229	4712	1153	120	1033	3679	36	12	102	86
1934	64·27	4843	316	4527	1060	93	967	3560	36	12	99	81
1935	64·81	4883	294	4589	1066	121	945	3644	33	11	110	86

PAT. NOS. 308794-22, 920069-22

HEAVY REPAIRS

DATE TAKEN OUT OF TRAFFIC	DATE PUT BACK INTO TRAFFIC	MILEAGE SINCE LAST HEAVY REPAIR	COST OF REPAIR REF. TO COST A/C.	COST OF REPAIR AMOUNT £
2·4·35	13·5·35	140 015	H.G. 713	1047 1066
7·4·36	24·4·36	76 787	H.S. 604	805

6000 LOCOMOTIVE ALLOTTED TO:—

DISTRICT	DATE FROM	DATE TO
35 Leeds	@ 30.10.33	
19 Longsight	16: 3·35.	
Leeds	25·7·36	

LIGHT REPAIRS

DATE TAKEN OUT OF TRAFFIC	DATE PUT BACK INTO TRAFFIC	MILEAGE SINCE LAST HEAVY OR LIGHT REPAIR	COST OF REPAIR REF. TO COST A/C.	COST OF REPAIR AMOUNT	
10·7·34	3·8·34	95 129	L.S. 1399	215	22
18·5·36	29·5·36	4 623	L.S. 855	27 *	11

* Includes £17·10·11 damaged in Collision

SUMMARY

YEAR	EXPENDITURE HEAVY REPAIRS £	LIGHT REPAIRS £	RUNNING REPAIRS AND SHED EXAMINATIONS £	TOTAL £	MILEAGE	COAL ISSUED (TONS)		WEEK DAYS OUT OF SERVICE HEAVY AND LIGHT REPAIRS	SHED REPAIRS AND EXAMINATIONS	NOT REQUIRED	TOTAL
1933	–		107	107	48 799	937	46	–	–	–	
1934	–	215	267	482	73 944	1507	46	22	46	8	76
1935	1077	–	268	1345	72 382	1443	45	35	28	8	71
1936	805	27	225	1057	72 698	1634	50	26	46	3	76

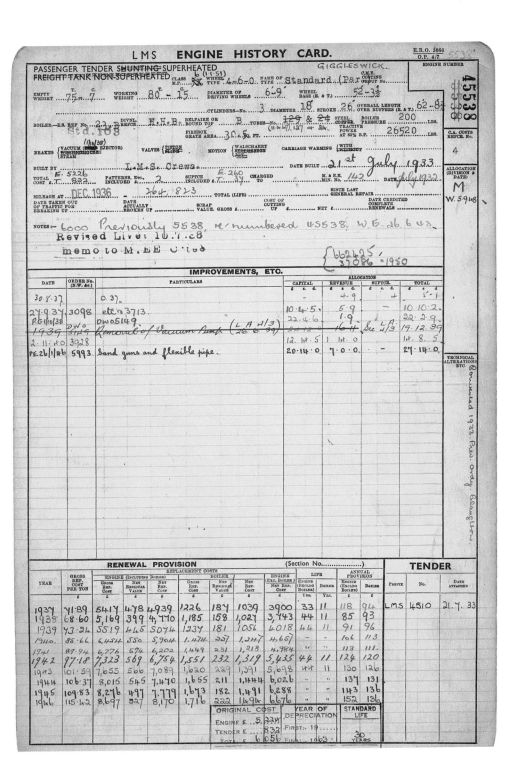

LMS **ENGINE HISTORY CARD.**

E.R.O. 3666
O.P. 4/7
5538'

ENGINE NUMBER: ~~5538~~ 45538

PASSENGER TENDER ~~SHUNTING~~ SUPERHEATED
~~FREIGHT TANK NON-SUPERHEATED~~

GIGGLESWICK.

CLASS M.P. ~~5X~~ 6 (1.1.51) WHEEL TYPE 4-6-0 NAME OF TYPE Standard (Par C.M.E. COSTING GROUP No.

EMPTY WEIGHT T. 75 C. 7 WORKING WEIGHT T. 80 C. 15 DIAMETER OF DRIVING WHEELS 6'-9" WHEEL BASE (E. & T.) 52-3½

CYLINDERS—No. 3 DIAMETER 18" STROKE 26" OVERALL LENGTH OVER BUFFERS (E. & T.) 62-8¾

BOILER.—E.S. REF No. 23 B DIVNL. REFCE. H.H.B. BELPAIRE OR ROUND TOP B TUBES—No. ~~129~~ & ~~24~~ (11.4.47) 127 & 24 STEEL ~~COPPER~~ BOILER PRESSURE 200 LBS.

Std. 103

FIREBOX GRATE AREA 30.5 FT. TRACTIVE POWER AT 85% B.P. 26520 LBS.

C.A. COSTS REFCE. No. 4

BRAKES {VACUUM (~~[illegible]~~ (1/10/38) EJECTOR) ~~WESTINGHOUSE~~ STEAM} VALVES {PISTON ~~SLIDE~~} MOTION {WALSCHAERT ~~STEPHENSON~~ ~~JOY~~} CARRIAGE WARMING {WITH ~~WITHOUT~~}

BUILT BY L.M.S. Crewe. DATE BUILT 21st July 1933

TOTAL COST £ E. 5226 T. 832 PATTERNS, ETC., INCLUDED £ 2 SUPTCE INCLUDED £ E. 260 T. 37 CHARGED TO M. & E.E. MIN. No. 142 DATE July 1932.

ALLOCATION (DIVISION & DATE) M W. 5.9.48

MILEAGE AT DEC. 1936 — 264,823 TOTAL (LIFE) SINCE LAST GENERAL REPAIR

DATE TAKEN OUT OF TRAFFIC FOR BREAKING UP DATE ACTUALLY BROKEN UP SCRAP VALUE. GROSS £ COST OF CUTTING UP £ NET £ DATE CREDITED COMPLETE RENEWALS

NOTES:— 6000 Previously 5538, re-numbered 45538, W.E. 26.6.48.
Revised Live: 10.7.58
memo to M.EE [illegible]
{662425, 37086 = 1950

IMPROVEMENTS, ETC.

DATE	ORDER No. (N.W. &c.)	PARTICULARS	CAPITAL £ s. d.	REVENUE £ s. d.	SUPTCE. £ s. d.	TOTAL £ s. d.
30.8.37.		O.37.	–	4.9.	4	5.1
27.9.37.	3098	etc 3713.	10.4.5.	5.9	–	10.10.2.
P.E.1/10/38	DWO	DWO5149	22.4.6	1.9		22.2.9.
~~1939~~	~~3149~~	~~Removal of Vacuum Pump (L.A. 4/3 26.6.39)~~	~~21.12.0~~	~~16.11~~	See L.A. 4/3	19.12.39
2.11.40	3928		12.14.5	1.14.0		14.8.5
P.E.26/1/46	5993	Sand guns and flexible pipe.	20.14.0	7.0.0.	–	27.14.0

TECHNICAL ALTERATIONS ETC.: Converted 1933. Prev. ordy. Claughton

RENEWAL PROVISION

(Section No.................)

YEAR	GROSS REP. COST PER TON £	ENGINE (Including Boiler) Gross Rep. Cost £	Net Residual Value £	Net Rep. Cost £	BOILER Gross Rep. Cost £	Net Residual Value £	Net Rep. Cost £	ENGINE (Exc. Boiler) Net Rep. Cost £	LIFE Engine (Excldg Boiler) Yrs.	Boiler Yrs.	ANNUAL PROVISION Engine (Excldg Boiler) £	Boiler £
1937	71.89	5417	478	4939	1226	187	1039	3900	33	11	118	94
1938	68.60	5,169	399	4,770	1,185	158	1,027	3,743	44	11	85	93
1939	73.24	5519	445	5074	1237	181	1056	4018	44	11	91	96
1940.	85.66	6,454	550	5,904	1,474	227	1,247	4,657	–	–	106	113
1941	89.94	6,776	574	6,202	1,449	231	1,218	4,984	"	"	113	111.
1942	97.18	7,323	569	6,754	1,551	232	1,319	5,435	44	11	124	120
1943	101.59	7,655	566	7,089	1,620	229	1,391	5,698	44	11	130	126
1944	106.37	8,015	545	7,470	1,655	211	1,444	6,026	"	"	137	131
1945	109.83	8,276	497	7,779	1,673	182	1,491	6,288	"	"	143	136
1946	115.42	8,697	527	8,170	1,716	222	1,494	6,676	"	"	152	136

ORIGINAL COST	YEAR OF DEPRECIATION	STANDARD LIFE
ENGINE £ 5,224	FIRST: 19.....	
TENDER £ 832		30 YEARS
TOTAL £ 6,056	FINAL 1963	

TENDER

PREFIX	No.	DATE ATTACHED
L.M.S	4510	21.7.33

BOILERS

FITTED / TAKEN OUT

DATE FITTED	REG'D No.	ECON. STOCK REFCE	BELF. R.T.	VALUE SHELL	VALUE FIREBOX	FROM	DATE NEW SHELL	DATE NEW FIREBOX	MILEAGE SHELL	MILEAGE FIREBOX	DATE RECOVERED	DISPOSAL	VALUE SHELL	VALUE FIREBOX	MILEAGE SHELL	MILEAGE FIREBOX
20.4.36		103	3	178	341	5975	1928	1936	260,946	—	20.4.36	Stock	92	179	307,702	76,787
10.9.37	5939	103	B.	176	232	5564	1932	1935	275,011	88,138	10.9.37	Stock	88	186	350,927	89,981
14.8.39	5370	103	B			5515										
19.10.40	6008					5518										
24.12.43	5369	W103	B			5533										
11.4.47	6007	103	B.			5530										
14.2.50	5977	103	B			5523										

HEAVY AND LIGHT REPAIRS

DATE TAKEN OUT OF TRAFFIC	DATE RETURNED TO TRAFFIC	No. OF WEEKDAYS OUT OF TRAFFIC	CLASS OF REPAIR	MILEAGE SINCE PREVIOUS HEAVY REPAIR — HEAVY	LIGHT	BOILER *	REPCH. TO COST A/C	TOTAL (R.O.3578)	REVENUE PORTION N.W. INCLUDED	NET ENGINE (EXCLUDG N.W. REV. & BOILER)	RECOV'D BOILER (EXCLUDG T. & M.)	TOTAL (ENGINE AND BOILER)
	13.5.35		H G									
7.4.36	24.4.36	15	H.S	76,787		2	604	805	—	557	87	
18.5.36	29.5.36	11	L.O.		4613			855	27	18 D	9	
29.3.37	30.5.37	54	H.S.	71,103		4	967	407	—	346	61	407
29.37	27.9.37	22	H.G.	18,878		2	1913	812	—	678	64	742
25.8.38	21.9.38	24	H.S.	77,047		2						
13.6.39	14.8.39	54	H G	57,684		2						
26.2.40	30.3.40	29	L.O.		43,788							
25.6.40	12.7.40	16	L.S		60,321							
25.9.40	19.10.40	22	H.O	48,094		2						
18.10.44	15.11.44		H.S.	65,442								
29.11.42	2.1.43	29	L.S.		52,825							
17.11.43	24.12.43	33	H.G.	104,543		2						
1.11.44	30.12.44	51	H.S.	51,721								
13.11.45	1.12.45	17	L.S.		39,739							
17.12.45	12.1.46	23	L.O.	91,929	40,210							
18.2.47	11.4.47	45	H.G.	88,077		2.C.						

MILEAGE SINCE PREVIOUS REPAIR	MILEAGE JAN. 1ST TO DATE SHOPPED
6.5.785	
62,413	20,076 C

26.5.48	22.6.48	24	L.S	65,785 / 62,413	20,076	C						
29.6.48	3.7.48	5	T.R.O.	—	—	C						
10.7.48	24.7.48	13	T.R.O.	—	—	C						

MILEAGE SINCE PREVIOUS GEN. OR INT.	NIL

14.12.49	14.2.50	44 / 26	H.G.	57,648	NIL	2.C.						
21.3.50	21.4.50	27	L.C.	5,903	5,903	C						
27.5.51	20.6.51	20	H.I.	53,422	16,336	C						
25.6.51	2.7.51	6	N.C.(Rest)	56	16,392	C						

BOILER

1 = NEW. 2 = CHANGED.
3 = LIFTED AND PUT BACK.
4 = REPAIRED ON FRAMES.

DISTRICT ALLOCATION

SHED	DATE
Leeds	25.7.36
Willesden (on loan)	21.8.48
Willesden	11.9.48
Edge Hill	28.5.49

STORED

SERVICEABLE OR UNSERV.	DATE IN	DATE OUT

SUMMARY

YEAR	REPAIRS EXPENDITURE HEAVY	LIGHT	RUNNING REPAIRS & SHEDS EXAMS.	TOTAL	MILEAGE	COAL ISSUED TONS	LBS. PER MILE	WEEKDAYS OUT OF SERVICE HEAVY & LIGHT REPAIRS	RUNNING REPAIRS & EXAMS.	OTHER PURPOSES	NOT REQUIRED	STORED SERVICEABLE	UNSERVICHABLE	TOTAL
1937	1219	-	147	1366	65,480	1454	50	76	27	-	5.	-	-	108
1938	(36 H.H.)	298		50,524										
(53 H.H.)					73,679	1480	45	24	67	-	3	-	-	94
1939					62,303			54	47	-	-	-	-	101
1940					59,368			67	10	-	1	-	-	78
1941					47,304			25	88	-	-	-	-	113
1942					44,097			23	93	-	1	-	-	117
1943					51,241			39	44	-	-	-	-	83
1944					51,790			51	49	-	-	-	-	100
1945					40,011			28	45	-	4	-	-	77
1946					46,779			12	71	-	3	-	-	86
1947					50,649			45	58	-	-	-	-	103
1948					35,197			42	61	-	3	-	-	106
1949					34,524			15	55	-	2	-	-	72
1950	37086				662,425 / (31.12.49)			55	41	-	-	-	-	96

B.R.   **ENGINE HISTORY CARD**   45538   E.R.O. 3666.

"GIGGLESWICK"

ENGINE NUMBER

45538

PASSENGER FREIGHT/MIXED TRAFFIC ~~TENDER TANK~~ SUPERHEATED NON-SUPERHEATER ~~DIESEL ELECTRIC MECHANICAL~~

	CLASS M.P. 6	WHEEL TYPE 4—6—0	NAME OF TYPE	PATRIOT STD. PAR.		

EMPTY WEIGHT T. 75 - C. 7   WORKING WEIGHT T. 80 - C. 15   DIAMETER OF DRIVING WHEELS 6' 9"   WHEEL BASE (E. & T.) 52' 3½"

CYLINDERS—No. 3   DIAMETER 18"   STROKE 26"   OVERALL LENGTH OVER BUFFERS (E. & T.) 62' 8¾"

C.A. COSTS REFCE. No.

BOILER.—E.S. REF. No. 103   DIVN'L REFCE G. 9½ S.   BELPAIRE OR ROUND TOP B   TUBES. No. 140-24 137 & 24   STEEL COPPER   BOILER PRESSURE 200 lbs.

BEARINGS, ROLLER—(Make)   FIREBOX GRATE AREA 30.5 SQ. FT.   TRACTIVE POWER AT 85% B.P. 26,520 lbs.

4

BRAKES VACUUM (PUMP EJECTOR) / ~~WESTINGHOUSE~~ / STEAM   VALVES PISTON ~~SLIDE POPPET~~   MOTION ~~CARROTTY~~ WALSCHAERT STEPHENSON ~~JOY GRESLEY~~   CARRIAGE WARMING WITH ~~WITHOUT~~

SPECIAL FEATURES :— Electric Light, Self-Cleaning Smokebox, Rocking Firegrate, Self-Emptying Ashpan, Manganese Steel Axlebox Liners.

DATE BUILT 21st July 1933

BUILT BY CREWE   LOT No.   REN'L PROG.   AUTHORITY :— Min. No. 142   DATE July 1932

MILEAGE AT 31.12.50   964,334   TOTAL (LIFE)   SINCE LAST GENERAL REPAIR

DATE TAKEN OUT OF TRAFFIC FOR BREAKING UP, ETC.   DATE ACTUALLY BROKEN UP 15th November 1962

NOTES :—

Withdrawn W.E. 22.9.62.

O/P. L.M.

ALLOCATION: Rectog. | Disp. Date | Region | Divn. | Date

IMPROVEMENTS, ETC.

DATE	ORDER No. (N.W. &c.)	PARTICULARS	ALLOCATION CAPITAL	REVENUE	TOTAL
24.12.52	E.2194	+ R. 1013 .	£ s. d. 10. 8. 4.	£ s. d. 11. 0. 10.	£ s. d. 13. 6
F.E. 31.10.59	E 4983	A.T.C.	302. 9. 0		802. 9. 0

DISTRICT ALLOCATION				ORIGINAL COST	YEAR OF DEPRECIATION	STANDARD LIFE	**TENDER**		
M.P. DEPOT	DATE	M.P. DEPOT	DATE				Prefix	No.	Date attached
Edge Hill	28.5.49			ENGINE £ 5224	FIRST :— 19___		LMS	4810	21.7.33
Preston	22.6.57			TENDER £ 832		30 Years	"	M558	23.8.56
Willesden	20.6.59			TOTAL £ 6,056	FINAL :— 19 62		"	3909	7.10.60
Nuneaton	14.1.61			Above information used for Depreciation purposes on and from 1/1/48.					

N/cf

CLASSIFIED REPAIRS (WORKSHOP AND M.P. DEPOT)
(* BOILER:—A=Changed, B=Lifted out and put back, C=Repaired on frames)

ENGINE NUMBER 45538

Taken out of traffic	Returned to traffic	Waiting Repair Decision	Waiting Works	On Works	Total	Class of Repair	Where repaired	Since previous General or Intermediate repair.	Jan. 1st to date shopped	* Boiler	Cost Form Serial No.	TOTAL as per cost form £	Revenue Portion of New Works included £
	4·2·50					HG	Crewe			A			
21·3·50	21·4·50				26	LC	"	5903	5903				
27·5·51	20·6·51	–	2	18	20	HI	"	53,422	16,336				
25·6·51	2·7·51	–	–	6	6	NC(Red)	"	57951 56 16,392					
26·9·52	20·12·52		12	61	73	HG	"	57,547 33,357	33,357	A			
19·1·53	9·3·53	5	13	24	42	LC	"	2540 1022	1022	B			
3·6·54	8·7·54	–	–	30	30	HI	"	56,989 15,738	15,738				
25·8·55	6·10·55	–	19	17	36	L.I.	"	57,2066257,048 31,004 31022					
9·12·56	26·2·57	5	7	53	65	HG.	"	53,312 40,457		A			
22·8·58	19·9·58	–	2	22	24	L.I.	"	66,509 26,927					
5·10·59	13·10·59	–	1	6	7	NC(EO)	"	45418 3257					
17·8·60	7·10·60	–	10	34	44	HI.	"	74,573 19,765					
11·10·60	19·10·60	–	–	7	7	NC(EO) 2nd	"	–	–				
25·10·60	27·10·60	–	–	2	2	NC(Rect EO)	"						

ANNUAL STATISTICS

Year	Mileage	Fuel Oil Issued (Gallons)	Waiting Repair Decision	Waiting Works	On Works	Total	Running Repairs & Exams.	Not Required	Serviceable	Unserviceable	Total
	964,334										
1951	40,726		–	2	24	26	34	–	–	–	60
1952	35,098		–	12	61	73	31				104
1953	41,734		5	13	24	42	41	–	–	–	83
1954	41,782		–	–	30	30	49				79
1955	43,877		–	19	17	36	39	14	–	–	89
1956	40,457		6	4	4	16	56	1	–	–	45
1957	39,582		–	–	49	49	51	–	–	–	100
1958	39,818		2	22	24	62	10				96
1959	41,914										
1960	28,803										
1961	20,486										
	1,378,594										

BOILER CHANGES

Date fitted	Registered No.	New or Repaired	Economic Stock Reference	Belpaire or Round Top
4·2·50	5977	R	103	B.
20·12·52	5984	R	103	B
26·2·57	5353	R	103	B

STORED (SERVICEABLE OR UNSERVICEABLE)

S. or U.S.	In	Out	S. or U.S.	In	Out
S	26·10·61	17·4·62			

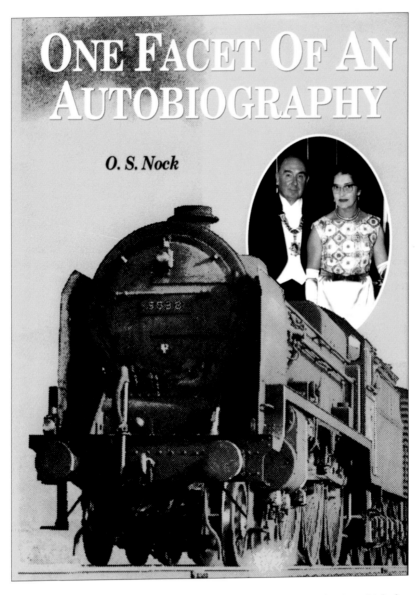

ONE FACET OF AN AUTOBIOGRAPHY

O. S. Nock

The cover of one of O. S. Nock's autobiographical works in which he provides an illuminating account of his life as an author. For the cover he has chosen an early profile of 'Giggleswick' and an insert photograph of him and his wife Olivia attending a function of the Institution of Railway Signal Engineers of which he was President in **1969-70.** *The Pentland Press.*

The scene at the Myers Grove School, Sheffield, on 14 June 2003 when the right nameplate of 'Giggleswick' came under the hammer at Sheffield Railwayana Auctions for £16,300. Mr Ian Wright is the auctioneer. *N.J. Mussett*

Former 'Giggleswick' fireman Don Rutter of Blackpool holds the original right nameplate above his head whilst resting one of the replica plates made from it on his lap. This photograph was taken at Giggleswick School in the summer of 2001. Sadly, Don died only a few months later. *Michael Robinson*

Former driver of 'Giggleswick' Edward Hickling in 2003. Having witnessed the naming of the locomotive in 1938 and driven it several times during his career on the railways, he was detailed to remove the right nameplate at Darnall depot, Sheffield, prior to the locomotive being scrapped in 1962. Edward retired in 1981. *N.J. Mussett*

Annual Mileage of LMS No. 5538 Giggleswick

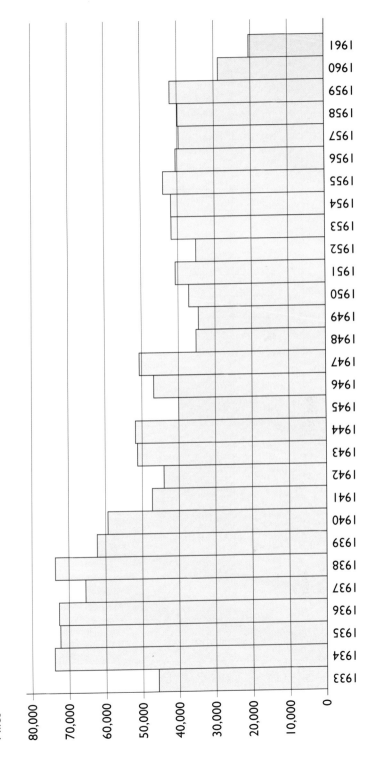

Miles

| 80,000 | 70,000 | 60,000 | 50,000 | 40,000 | 30,000 | 20,000 | 10,000 | 0 |

1961
1960
1959
1958
1957
1956
1955
1954
1953
1952
1951
1950
1949
1948
1947
1946
1945
1944
1943
1942
1941
1940
1939
1938
1937
1936
1935
1934
1933

The locomotive *Giggleswick*: percentage of days per year in service

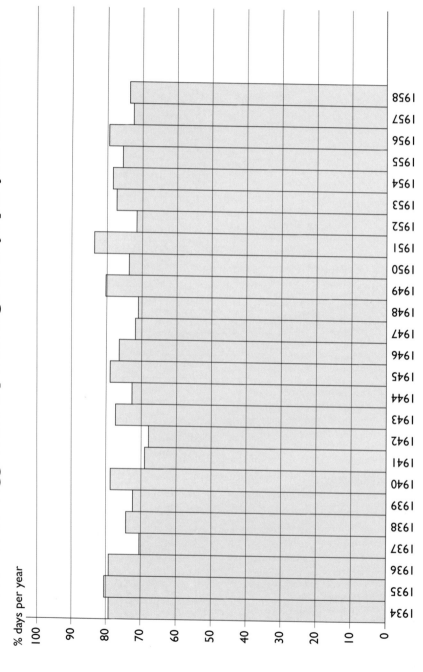

% days per year

100 90 80 70 60 50 40 30 20 10 0

1934 1935 1936 1937 1938 1939 1940 1941 1942 1943 1944 1945 1946 1947 1948 1949 1950 1951 1952 1953 1954 1955 1956 1957 1958

3. Working for British Railways 1948-1962

Giggleswick was still based at Leeds Holbeck shed when the railways were nationalised under the post-war Labour government on 1 January 1948. This was near the half-way point in *Giggleswick's* life and after receiving her new British Railways number of 45538 in June of that year she was sent on loan to Willesden depot (shed code 1A) in north west London on 21 August 1948, becoming permanently allocated there on 11 September. A further move came on 28 May of the following year when she went north again, this time to Edge Hill depot (code 8A) in Liverpool.

The locomotive was still to be seen in 1946 LMS passenger livery until well into 1949 when it was photographed picking up water from Whitmore Troughs. It is apparent in this striking photograph that the new BR number only had been applied to the cab side, the LMS lettering being retained on the tender for some time afterwards and possibly the rest of the locomotive being left in LMS lined black. No photographs of *Giggleswick* have been found by the author showing the title 'British Railways' borne on the sides of the tender as indicated on the Hornby Gauge 00 model and it seems unlikely that the locomotive ever appeared in this guise. However, black tenders attached to some of the 'Patriot' Class (mostly those, it seems, that had been rebuilt with the 2A tapered boiler) certainly did carry this wording. Soon, however, another attempt at corporate identity was undertaken by applying to the tenders the first type of the BR emblem, dating from 1948, depicting a lion straddling a wheel and disparagingly termed the 'ferret and dartboard' by some railwaymen. The first photographs of *Giggleswick* shown here of the tender bearing this emblem date from between 28 May 1949 and the end of 1950; engine and tender would by now rather belatedly have been repainted and finished off in BR lined black gloss.

Following this, in the first half of the 1950s, most passenger locomotives were then repainted in BR Brunswick Green, lined in orange and black. The accompanying green tenders were embellished with a second and altogether more aesthetically pleasing heraldic emblem which had been officially granted to the British Transport Commission by the College of Arms and the Lyon Office of Scotland in 1956. *Giggleswick* seems to have adopted these

A much-used image of *Giggleswick* heading the down St Pancras to Glasgow St Enoch restaurant car express on 15 May 1948. This photograph was taken at Radlett Aerodrome, south of St Albans, on the former Midland Railway main line to the north. The new British Railways number had not yet been applied following nationalisation. *E.D. Bruton/Mark Hoofe Collection*

A neat profile of a fresh looking BR No. 45538 at an undisclosed location. Another photograph of the locomotive taken at the same time but from a different angle shows the shed code as 8A (Edge Hill, Liverpool) and the power class on the cab side is shown as 5XP. This dates the photograph between 28 May 1949 and the end of 1950. The first BR emblem had by now been applied to the tender, both engine and tender being finished in BR lined black at this time. *David Parry Collection*

changes soon after this time. The nameplates were painted black again for this final phase. These changes can be followed in the photographs taken as she performed her various duties around the country.

Between 1946 and 1948 eighteen 'Patriot' Class locomotives had been selected for rebuilding using the larger Stanier Type 2A tapered boiler; the programme was completed shortly after nationalisation. Derek Cross (1982) claims that this conversion 'made a good engine even better'. The tractive effort achieved with this boiler in these locomotives rose to 29,590lb, a considerable improvement over the 26,520lb of the unrebuilt 'Patriots'. The cab was redesigned and the engines also acquired an enlarged Stanier 4,000-gallon tender, making them very similar in appearance to a rebuilt 'Royal Scot'. Shortly after their rebuilding, both 'Royal Scots' and the eighteen 'Patriots' were given curved smoke deflectors. When these rebuilt main line locomotives were subsequently upgraded, along with the 'Jubilees', to Class 7 the unrebuilt 'Patriots' were themselves upgraded to Class 6 from 5X. For BR 45538 *Giggleswick*, this change came in November 1951.

It was whilst allocated to Edge Hill depot that *Giggleswick* received her second tender, No. 4558, on 23 August 1956, parting with the one which had accompanied her for the first twenty three years of her working life. After six years operating out of Edge Hill *Giggleswick* was then reallocated to Preston motive power depot (code 10B, changed to 24K in 1958) on 22 June 1957 for two years, after which she was sent back to London for a further stint at Willesden on 20 June 1959. Her tender from Edge Hill was exchanged for a final one, No. 3909, on 7 October 1960. Whilst in BR service *Giggleswick* was fitted with three further replacement parallel boilers.

Under the modernisation plan of British Railways in the mid-1950s the policy of replacing steam traction was soon put into effect: by the early 1960s the last of BR's steam locomotives had been built and powerful new classes of diesel and electric locomotives were appearing across the network. Along with the 'Royal Scots', 'Jubilees' and some other larger locomotive types, the 'Patriots' continued to give faithful service in all areas on both passenger and freight duties towards the end of their lives. Frequently seen hauling express services over the main lines of the Midland Region of British Railways, *Giggleswick* also undertook a variety of other duties as the assemblage of photographs in this chapter portrays.

For the 'Patriots' the end came quickly. The first withdrawals late in 1960 were of BR Nos 45502 and 45508. Only eleven engines survived into 1964

An interesting shot of *Giggleswick* taking water from the Whitmore watertroughs on the former LNWR west coast main line between Crewe and Stafford in 1949. Heading the down North Wales express, the locomotive is bearing the new British Railways cab side number of 45538 on an area of paintwork prepared for the purpose. The tender, however, still displays the pre-nationalisation initials of the LMS. Both engine and tender at this time are apparently still in LMS post-war 1946 black livery. *Gordon Tidey Collection/National Railway Museum*

BR No. 45538 *Giggleswick* **hauls a down express through Slaithwaite station on the former LNWR line between Manchester and Huddersfield c. 1950. The locomotive was still black at this time and the leading coach has been painted in the new red and cream livery of British Railways.** *Kenneth Field/Rail Archive Stephenson*

Giggleswick is shown working hard as she emerges from Standedge Tunnel on the Manchester-Huddersfield-Leeds line with a down express c. 1951. Of equal interest is the seemingly casual approach to health and safety issues on the railways at the time. *Kenneth Field/Rail Archive Stephenson*

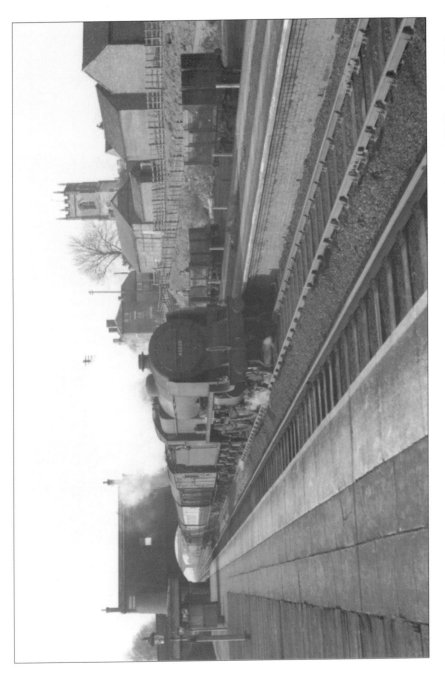

Still operating from 8A Edge Hill depot, *Giggleswick* is here caught passing through the former LNWR station of Shilton with a local train on the west coast main line between Crewe and Rugby on 15 March 1951. Drivers apparently checked their timings against the church clock! The station closed in September 1957. *Alec Ford*

BR No. 45538 *Giggleswick* lying idle at Crewe works on 30 June 1951 when she was out of service for six days for repairs. The new power classification of 6P is shown above the number on the cab side although according to the Engine History Card this was not officially designated until November of that year. *W.L. Good/Mark Hoofe Collection*

This photograph, taken at Birmingham New Street Station in the early-mid 1950s, shows a smart *Giggleswick* waiting to depart. *Stephenson Locomotive Society/David Parry Collection*

BR No. 45538 *Giggleswick* between duties at Longsight depot, near Manchester, on 15 March 1953. *M.N. Bland/Transport Treasury*

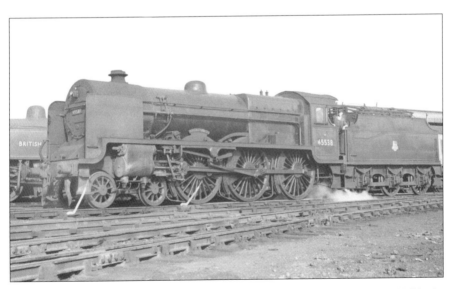

BR No. 45538 *Giggleswick* waiting for her next duty at Watford in July 1953. At this time, the engine was allocated to Edge Hill depot (8A) in Liverpool. *J. Robertson/Transport Treasury*

Giggleswick hauling a long passenger express through Shrewsbury in the mid-1950s. The coaches shown here were painted in the maroon livery of the Midland Region. *Locofotos*

BR No. 45538 *Giggleswick* ready to depart with her next train from Shrewsbury Station, **1954.** *Locofotos*

Another photograph of *Giggleswick* at Shrewsbury, this time "on shed" awaiting her next duty in 1955. At this time she was still based at 8A Edge Hill depot. *Locofotos*

A dramatic picture of BR No. 45538 *Giggleswick* taking water from the Castlethorpe troughs near Wolverton on 7 May 1955. In their latter days passenger locomotives such as the 'Patriots' and 'Royal Scots' were increasingly rostered to carry freight traffic such as this down set of empty milk wagons. The tender shown here had accompanied *Giggleswick* since she entered service in 1933; it was replaced by a tender of similar design in August 1956. *D.M.C. Hepburne-Scot/Rail Archive Stephenson*

and only three did so into 1965. It will be recalled that the last 'Patriot' in service, rebuilt No. 45530 *Sir Frank Ree*, was withdrawn at the end of December 1965. Constructed three months before *Giggleswick* in 1933, this locomotive in 1946 was the first of the eighteen 'Patriots' to be rebuilt with the 2A tapered boiler and was apparently kept in particularly good condition until nearly the end of her life (Sixsmith, 2003), by which time she had covered a staggering total of approximately 1,740,000 miles. Arguably, this locomotive would have been an obvious candidate for preservation as representative of its class.

Giggleswick undertook her last operational tasks from Nuneaton depot (shed code 2B) to which she had been allocated on 14 January 1961. By the time she appeared there she had travelled over 1.35 million miles and had served twenty seven and a half of her expected standard life of thirty years. During 1960 she had only travelled 28,803 miles, by far the lowest annual mileage since she entered service and so it was only a matter of time before she was withdrawn. No maintenance or repair works are recorded after 1960. Only 20,486 miles were covered during 1961 up to the point when she was put into store at Rugby depot on 26 October. Eleven months later

Still operating out of Edge Hill motive power depot, BR No. 45538 *Giggleswick* basks in the sun at an undisclosed depot, probably in the mid-1950s. *Locofotos*

she was taken out of service and officially withdrawn during the week ending 22 September 1962, outside of the programme (the "O/P" on the History Card) of the London Midland Region, never to steam again. Throughout her working life *Giggleswick* had notched up a total of 1,378,594 miles – an average of 48,800 miles per year. This was quite an impressive record as the two prototype 'Patriots', LMS Nos 5500 and 5501, had totalled 1,239,904 and 1,266,776 miles respectively, representing annual averages of only 40,989 and 41,140 miles during their days as 'Patriots'.

Soon after this *Giggleswick* was towed away for breaking up, the actual date of which is officially recorded as being 15 November 1962, but her exact movements are uncertain. Many references state that she was scrapped at Crewe works: possibly a fleeting visit was made there to salvage some useful components but documentation is lacking. For the first time it can be placed on record for certain that the actual cutting up was undertaken in Sheffield. On her arrival in the city, *Giggleswick* was taken to Darnall motive power depot where Edward Hickling and his colleague were detailed to remove the nameplates. If the locomotive had, in fact, gone to Crewe, it would be surprising if the nameplates had not been removed there.

Awaiting another turn of duty at an undisclosed location c. mid-1950s whilst allocated to Edge Hill depot. *David Parry Collection*

Giggleswick **Driver Jimmy Hardy with young enthusiast David Howarth on the platform at Blackpool North Station in 1957.** *David Howarth Collection*

An interesting picture of *Giggleswick* taking on coal at the depot in Preston, August 1957. *Transport Treasury*

Giggleswick is pictured at Crewe South shed on 23 August 1958. The shed code plate on the firebox door is 24K, the new code that year for Preston, which had previously been 10B. *R.A. Savill/David Parry Collection*

In any event, BR No. 45538 *Giggleswick* was finally towed unceremoniously the short distance from Darnall depot to the private scrap yard of Thomas Ward on the Rotherham Road for cutting up. Edward Hickling went there to pay his last respects to his favourite locomotive, the one he had seen named at Settle Station exactly twenty four years previously, and which he had both cleaned, fired and driven on many occasions, including one memorable run when he was in charge of the 'Thames-Clyde Express'. 'She was a lovely smooth rider,' he recalls to this day. 'One of the best.'

Not one 'Patriot' locomotive survived the cutter's torch for preservation. It was a sad end to a successful and well-respected class of locomotive. Essery and Jenkinson (1989) wrote that '...more than most classes, the 'Patriots' ...did all that was ever required of them...this is what the LMS most wanted of its engines and is, perhaps, their most fitting epitaph'.

The scene at Farington Station, south of Preston, on Saturday 13 June 1959 with *Giggleswick* thundering through with a Blackpool Central to Bletchley holiday train. It is interesting to note that the shed code 1A (Willesden) appears on the smokebox door but the Engine History Card indicates that allocation to that depot from Preston did not take place until a week later, 20 June. *D.T. Greenwood/Rail Archive Stephenson*

Fireman Don Rutter oils the motion on 19 August 1961 while Driver 'Tug' Wilson looks on between summer Saturday duties at Rigby Road, Blackpool. Bearing the code of her final shed allocation 2B Nuneaton, *Giggleswick* had by now only two months left in service. Also seen here is the last of the three 3,500-gallon tenders carried by the locomotive during her working life. *Don Rutter Collection*

One of the last photographs of *Giggleswick* in service before being put in store at Rugby depot. This scene was captured at Crewe South shed on 6 September 1961. *Norman Preedy Archive*

Work on the west coast main line electrification is in progress whilst BR No. 45538 *Giggleswick* pauses at Stafford Station in 1961. *Norman Preedy Archive*

Stripped of her shed allocation plate, *Giggleswick* waits in the line-up of locomotives in store at Rugby depot in November 1961. The covered-up funnels also indicated that the locomotives were not attached or commissioned to a particular depot. *Locofotos*

Giggleswick seen again at Rugby motive power depot where she was in store from 26 October 1961 until 17 September 1962 prior to being officially withdrawn in the week ending 22 September. Despite the coal in the tender, the engine was unlikely ever to have been fired again. From here she was towed for cutting up in Sheffield, but not before her number and nameplates had been removed at Darnall depot. *Locofotos*

4. The Nameplates

Giggleswick received her brass nameplates shortly before the naming ceremony at Settle Station on the wet afternoon of 4 November 1938. In order to ensure the correct fitting of engine nameplates, identification marks were made (probably by drilling) into the back of the castings, one mark being made into the left nameplate and two marks into the right one.

When the nameplates were first mounted to a backplate on the leading wheel splashers in 1938, the locomotive *Giggleswick* was painted crimson and the nameplates were black. When the engine received the post-war LMS black livery the nameplate background would have been maroon and finally, when the engine received its BR green livery, the nameplate was once again painted black. One can only conjecture what shade of red the nameplates were during the early BR black livery phase.

Edward Hickling recalls that the right nameplate was boxed up and sent to Giggleswick School after he had removed it at Darnall depot, Sheffield. Apparently, this plate had been reserved by Mr G.B. Gray, the Divisional Passenger Manager of British Railways in the East Midlands. Mr Gray had a son at the school at the time and was keen to present the school with one of the nameplates when the locomotive came to be withdrawn. Particular significance was attached to this right nameplate as it was the one over which the bottle of champagne had been broken by the Headmaster in November 1938. Soon after its arrival at the school it was repainted maroon and mounted above the doorway of the dining room in the main Hostel building. There it remained until 1999 when the dining room and adjacent kitchens were redeveloped to create a new library area. Realising its potential value, the school locked the nameplate away in a safe, taking it out occasionally for brass replicas to be made from it and sold for £250 each. After the castings had been made, the nameplate was restored and, like the replicas made from it, had the background painted bright red. One of these replicas was mounted in the entrance foyer at the school, only a few metres away from the former position of the original nameplate above the dining room entrance. Another was presented by the school to the Friends of the Settle-Carlisle Line at a brief ceremony held at the school on 6 June 2003. This replica plate was subsequently delivered to Settle Station for mounting on a board featuring the locomotive and its naming there sixty five years earlier.

The recent sales by other public schools of artefacts and works of art had prompted the Governors to consider auctioning the nameplate in their possession. It had been suggested that it could fetch a sum in excess of £40,000 in auction but what basis there was for considering such a sum is hard to imagine. Informed opinion considered even half this figure to be somewhat optimistic. When the decision to auction the nameplate was finally announced in 2002 it was opposed by several past and present members of the school who felt that such assets, being part of the school's heritage, should remain firmly in its possession and especially as this particular artefact had been presented to the school in the first place. In defence, the Governors stated that, as Trustees of the school Charity, they had a duty to consider whether retention of valuable assets was in accordance with the objects of the Charity which, after all, were primarily concerned with the education of pupils. The son of Mr Gray was contacted regarding this decision.

And so, the nameplate was finally offered to Sheffield Railwayana Auctions for sale on Saturday 14 June 2003. The sale catalogue listed the nameplate as Lot No. 400 but gave no valuation. Hundreds of railway enthusiasts had converged on the Myers Grove School for the auction on what turned out to be a bright summer's day. Numerous traders had set up their stalls and the auction began at 11.00a.m. in a blistering heat. After a break for lunch and with the temperature still rising, the lively auction resumed with lot No. 301. The *Giggleswick* nameplate came up soon after 3.00p.m. Bidding started at £14,000. The auctioneer, Mr Ian Wright, asked if anyone from the school was present in the hall; in fact at least two Old Boys and two former staff had turned up to witness the sale. Within a few minutes the bidding had ceased at £16,300 and it was all over, the buyer being a Kent-based businessman. The nameplate had been sold for approximately the price expected by the railway fraternity and less than half the figure suggested to the Governors. In fact, the price realised proved to be less than a single boarding fee for that year and a vital part of the school's heritage had been lost for ever.

It was perhaps a sad irony that Sheffield should have been the location both of the breaking up of the locomotive and the sale of one of its remaining nameplates.

As for the left nameplate, so far as I can trace, nothing has been heard or seen of it since it was removed by Edward Hickling's colleague at Darnall depot and sent for sale, possibly in Leeds, in November 1962. The Sheffield

Presentation of a replica right nameplate by Giggleswick School to the Friends of the Settle-Carlisle Line on 6 June 2003. Left to right: Philip Johnston (Chairman of the Friends), Geoffrey Boult (Headmaster of Giggleswick School) and Glynn Hague (Vice-Chairman of the Friends). *N. J. Mussett*

The *Giggleswick* commemorative board at Settle Station unveiled in December 2003 showing the replica nameplate presented to the Friends of the Settle-Carlisle Line, accompanied by photographs and brief historical notes. *N.J. Mussett*

auction catalogue stated that 'the other nameplate is not known'; it is likely to have been preserved somewhere, probably concealed in a private collection. For the time being, however, members of the public will have to be content with the replica nameplates, models, photographs and various publications to keep alive the proud memories of Giggleswick's locomotive.

A final reminder for members of Giggleswick School. The right nameplate mounted prominently above the entrance to the old dining hall at the school from 1962 to 1999. During this time it had been repainted in LMS crimson in between the lettering. *David Parry*

References

Allen, C.J. 1949. The Last of the 'Claughtons'. *Trains Illustrated,* August-September, pp. 71-77.

Anderson, D. 1992. The 'Patriots' and Their Nameplates. *Steam World,* **55,** January, pp. 14-19.

Anon. 1938. Speech Day 1938. Report in *Giggleswick School Chronicle,* **176,** July 1938, pp. 206-212. Reprinted from *The Craven Herald.*

Anon. 1938. Our Engine. Article in *Giggleswick School Chronicle,* **177,** December 1938, pp. 267-268.

Anon. 1939. Photograph and notes on the naming of LMS 5538 'Giggleswick' at Settle, November 1938. *LMS Magazine,* 1939, p. 45.

Aves, W.A.T. 1997. LMS 'Patriots'. *Steam Days.* March, pp. 178-189.

Cross, D. 1982. The 'Claughtons' and 'Patriots'. *Locomotives Illustrated,* **27,** pp. 4-38.

Essery, B. and Jenkinson, D. 1981. *An Illustrated History of LMS Locomotives.* Volume 1. Oxford Publishing Co., Oxford.

Essery, B. and Jenkinson, D. 1989. *An Illustrated History of LMS Locomotives: The Post-grouping Standard Designs.* Volume 5. Silver Link Publishing, Kettering.

Jenkinson, D. and Essery, B. 1967. *Locomotive Liveries of the LMS.* Roundhouse/Ian Allan, London.

McLoughlin, B. 2001. Article on Fireman Don Rutter in *Steam World,* November, p.6.

Nock, O.S. 1974. The Locomotive 'Giggleswick'. *Giggleswick School Chronicle*, **283**, Winter 1974, pp. 16-17.

Nock, O.S. 1978. *The Royal Scots and Patriots of the LMS*. David and Charles, Newton Abbot.

Nock, O.S. 1989. *Great Locomotives of the LMS*. Patrick Stephens, Wellingborough.

Nock, O.S. 1992. *One Facet of an Autobiography*. The Pentland Press, Durham.

Pearce, D. 2001. Article in the 'Memory Lane' series, *The Blackpool Gazette*, featuring 'Giggleswick' and Don Rutter. 12 June 2001.

Powell, A.J. 1992. Were the 'Patriots' really necessary? *Steam Days*, **34**, June, pp. 307-311 & 330.

Romans, M. 1989. The Rebuilt 'Royal Scots', 'Patriots' and 'Jubilees'. *Locomotives Illustrated*, **68**, pp. 4-13.

Rowledge, J.W.P. 2003. The LMS Three-Cylinder '5XP' & '6P' Passenger Classes. *Locomotives Illustrated*, **150**, July-August, pp. 4-45.

Sixsmith, I. 2003. *The Book of the Patriot 4-6-0s*. Irwell Press, Bedford.

http://www.itnarchive.com
>   This video comprises a 21-second black-and-white British Pathe newsreel film clip with voice-over commentary and showing the naming ceremony at Settle Station on 4 November 1938. The ITN Archive has now incorporated the British Pathe news film archive.

http://www.st-dunstans.org.uk
>   A website providing historical notes, news and support details. Archive and photo-library facilities are also available.

Giggleswick School

The origins of Giggleswick School can be traced to pre-Reformation days, growing out of the grammar school class run by the local chantry priest associated with the ancient parish church of St Alkelda in Giggleswick. Following the Reformation, the school was established as a royal grammar school foundation under Edward VI, receiving its charter in 1553, but still remaining closely associated with the village and its church. Coincidentally, the school moved to its present site in the village during the 1870s at the same time as the Settle-Carlisle line was being built.

The school accepted Sixth Form girls in 1976 and went fully co-educational in 1983. There are at present 470 pupils in the senior and junior parts of the school with a further 30 in the pre-preparatory department. It maintains its position as one of the leading independent co-educational boarding schools in the north of England. A broad and modern curriculum is offered to all pupils; there is a strong tradition of music, drama and extra-curricular activities in addition to the varied sports and service activities on offer. Being situated in the heart of the Yorkshire Dales, outdoor education has for nearly a century played a key role in helping to inculcate an interest in the natural world as well as providing opportunities for developing initiative, self-reliance and leadership amongst it pupils.

Giggleswick School, Settle, North Yorkshire. BD24 0DE
(Tel. 01729 893000) http://www.giggleswick.org.uk

The Author

Nigel Mussett has had a life-long interest in railways. Initially a botanist by training but subsequently also obtaining degrees in history and educational research, he has spent the whole of his teaching career as a secondary school Head of Biology, the last twenty nine years of which were at Giggleswick School. During this time he ran a popular Railway Society and was also Secretary of the Settle-Carlisle Railway Centenary Committee set up by the then Settle Civic Society to work closely with British Rail, local authorities and many others to co-ordinate events in 1976 celebrating the centenary of the opening of the line to passenger traffic. He is a Life Member of the Friends of the National Railway Museum and a member of the Friends of the Settle-Carlisle Line. He has also served as a Chief Examiner in GCE Biology for many years as well as being involved in nature conservation and work with the Royal Life Saving Society. He was appointed MBE (Military) in 2001 for his work with the cadet forces and has been elected to Fellowship of both the Institute of Biology and the Linnean Society of London.

In 1976 he was co-author with W.R. Mitchell of *Seven Years Hard* which gave a year-by-year account of the building of the Settle-Carlisle line. He is married and lives in Giggleswick.

Cover Illustrations
Front: **LMS 5538 *Giggleswick* hauling the down 'Thames-Forth Express' along Dentdale.** *Reproduced with permission from a painting by Paul Gribble, one of eight in a series of Great Steam Trains depicted on plates produced by Davenport China, in association with O.S. Nock, 1990. Copyright: Bradford Exchange.*
Back: **Three versions of a limited edition Gauge 00 Hornby-based model of *Giggleswick*, commissioned by Giggleswick School in 1999.** *N.J. Mussett*